SCHOLASTI

Math Games
to Master Basic Skills
MULTIPLICATION & DIVISION

by Denise Kiernan

Dedication

For Joe

Edited by Irving Crump and Immacula A. Rhodes
Cover design by Jason Robinson
Interior illustrations by Teresa Anderko
Interior design by Sydney Wright

ISBN-13: 978-0-439-51773-7
ISBN-10: 0-439-51773-7

3 4 5 6 7 8 9 10   40   14 13 12 11 10 09 08

NEW YORK • TORONTO • LONDON • AUCKLAND • SYDNEY
MEXICO CITY • NEW DELHI • HONG KONG • BUENOS AIRES

Teaching *Resources*

Contents

Introduction

Math Games to Master Basic Skills: Multiplication & Division provides fun, familiar games that help students master basic facts. The games in this book, variations of well-known childhood games such as Bingo, War!, Go Fish!, Concentration, Tic-Tac-Toe, and Checkers, will engage and motivate students while reinforcing their ability to compute basic facts with accuracy and fluency.

The National Council of Teachers of Mathematics (NCTM) defines computational fluency as the "connection between conceptual understanding and computational proficiency." Learning the basic facts to the point of automaticity plays a key role in helping students successfully work with higher-level multiplication and division problems. You can use these math games to increase students' fluency in using basic facts and help equip them with essential tools to perform higher-level operations with whole-number combinations. The games are ideal for students who need extra reinforcement and repeated practice to strengthen their mastery of the basic skills they need to know.

In *Math Games to Master Basic Skills: Multiplication & Division*, you'll find all the materials needed to play the different versions of each game. All the games are easy to assemble and can be tailored to fit the needs of individual students, small or large groups, or the entire class.

There are a variety of ways you can use these versatile games with students. Invite students to use the games in learning centers, during free-choice time, before or after school, as class warm-ups, or when they have finished other tasks. You can also send the games home for students to play with family and friends. The variation for each game suggests an additional way to use elements of the game to build and reinforce students' skills and interest.

Math Games to Master Basic Skills: Multiplication & Division is the perfect tool to help your students master the basic facts—an all-important skill that will put them on the road to math success in future years!

How to Use This Book

Math Games to Master Basic Skills: Multiplication & Division includes the following:

* An introduction page for each of the six games (pages 8–13): The information on this page includes the game objective, number of players, different versions for playing the game, the materials needed, and directions on how to play the game. For all the games except Checkers, variations are provided to suggest additional ways to use the games to build and reinforce students' skills and interest. In addition, a challenge activity is included for each game to help students develop an understanding of the inverse property of multiplication and division operations.

❋ Reproducible game boards for Bingo and Tic-Tac-Toe (pages 14–16): This book contains two game boards for Bingo (one for multiplication and the other for division) and one for Tic-Tac-Toe. Each of the game boards contains blank boxes so that you can customize them to target the specific skills you'd like students to work on. Directions for preparing the Bingo game boards are found on page 6. By preparing the game boards in advance, you'll have them ready to use anytime students have an opportunity to play them.

❋ Reproducible game cards (pages 17–35): The game cards are essential components of all the games except Checkers. Each set of 12 game cards features a multiplication or division fact family from 1–12, or the related products or quotients. To use, simply decide which operation and fact family you'd like to feature in a game. Then locate the corresponding game cards and prepare them as directed for the selected game (see page 5).

❋ Reproducible game markers (page 35): For your convenience, game markers are provided for use with Bingo, Tic-Tac-Toe, and Checkers. Copy, laminate, and cut out the number of game markers needed for each player for each game. Be sure to use the specific paper colors indicated in the directions for Tic-Tac-Toe and Checkers.

❋ Reproducible caller recording charts (pages 36–43): These charts are for use with the multiplication and division Bingo games. According to the version of the game being played, the caller selects and calls out specific facts, products, or quotients from the chart, making sure to mark off each item as it is called. The marked chart can be used to check players' answers and help determine the winner of the game. For durability and reusability, laminate each of the charts. Then have the caller use a wipe-off marker to mark the items. When finished, clean the chart with a paper towel for use again in future games.

❋ Reproducible Checkers game boards (pages 44–47): An easy-to-assemble game board is provided for each of the operations featured in this book: multiplication and division. Each game board contains either mixed multiplication or division facts and is designed to reinforce students' mastery of these facts.

Choosing a Version of the Game to Play

There are many different ways you can customize the games in *Math Games to Master Basic Skills: Multiplication & Division*. This versatility lies in the flexible use of the game boards and game cards.

Near the top of the introduction page for each game that uses the game cards, you'll find a "Choose a Version to Play" section. You can refer to this section to help you decide how students might use the cards to play the game and which game cards to use for the game. For each game, you'll need to target which specific fact family or families you want to emphasize. Some versions allow you to feature only one fact family, while others let you feature up to three fact families. After you become familiar with the different game versions, formats, and materials, you may want to mix and match the facts in each game to meet the specific needs of your students or to provide them with more opportunities and challenges to master these facts. You might also discover other ways to use the games to interest and motivate students.

Here's an example to help you understand how one version of Bingo might be played: Let's say you want players to find the multiplication problems for the 4's and 5's fact families that equal specific products. For this version, players will use the prepared multiplication Bingo game cards that feature the 4's and 5's fact families (label the game boards with this information). The caller will use the corresponding caller recording charts found on page 37. To play, the caller calls out any product (shown in a circle) on one of the caller recording charts. He or she then marks off that space and all others containing facts equal to that product. Players search their game boards for any multiplication facts that equal the named product and cover each one with a game marker.

For your convenience, the following chart is provided as a reference to help you locate the game cards or caller recording charts for specific multiplication or division facts.

Fact Family	Multiplication (Page)	Division (Page)
Game Cards: 1's & 2's Facts	17	29
Game Cards: 3's & 4's Facts	18	30
Game Cards: 5's & 6's Facts	19	31
Game Cards: 7's & 8's Facts	20	32
Game Cards: 9's & 10's Facts	21	33
Game Cards: 11's & 12's Facts	22	34
Game Cards: Products for 1's & 2's Facts	23	
Game Cards: Products for 3's & 4's Facts	24	
Game Cards: Products for 5's & 6's Facts	25	
Game Cards: Products for 7's & 8's Facts	26	
Game Cards: Products for 9's & 10's Facts	27	
Game Cards: Products for 11's & 12's Facts	28	
Game Cards: Quotients		35
Caller Recording Chart: 1's–3's Facts	36	40
Caller Recording Chart: 4's–6's Facts	37	41
Caller Recording Chart: 7's–9's Facts	38	42
Caller Recording Chart: 10's–12's Facts	39	43

How to Prepare and Use the Games

Each set of game cards on pages 17–35 can be used to play all the games in the book except Checkers. For Bingo, the game cards are glued onto the multiplication or division Bingo game boards. The Tic-Tac-Toe game board is used as a placeholder for the game cards. In War!, Go Fish!, and Concentration, the cards serve as individual playing cards. Follow the directions on pages 6–7 to prepare each game for use.

Bingo

By creating your own Bingo board games, you have the flexibility to customize each game to fit students' needs. You can feature one or two specific fact families or a wide range of facts on the game boards. You can also decide whether you want to make enough game boards for whole-class use, large or small groups, or pairs. Solicit the help of students or volunteers to create a class supply of the game boards for the different fact families. Or have individual students make their own game boards that feature the specific facts they need to work on.

1. For a class supply of the game boards, choose the version of the game students will play, the mathematical operation, and the specific fact families you want to feature. Copy for each student the game board that corresponds to the selected operation: page 14 for multiplication and page 15 for division. Also copy the game cards that feature the selected fact families (refer to the chart on page 5). You'll need two pages of cards for every three students.

2. Distribute the game boards. Have students color the border of their game boards and write the fact families on the line.

3. Give every three students two pages of game cards. Have them cut out and place the 48 cards facedown in a random array. Then ask students to pick 16 cards each. Have them glue each card faceup on a blank space on their game board.

4. Collect all the game boards. Then copy a set of 12 game markers for each student. Laminate the game boards, game markers, and a copy of the corresponding caller recording charts for the fact families featured on the game boards. Cut out all the game pieces.

5. Store the game pieces in a large resealable plastic bag. Label the bag with the skill featured on the game boards. Also include a wipe-off pen and paper towels.

To mix it up a bit, you might want to create game boards that feature both multiplication and division facts. If you do this, be sure to write the skills on the game boards and storage bag, and include copies of all the related caller recording charts.

War!, Go Fish!, and Concentration

To prepare for these games, choose the version you want students to play and the specific facts you'd like to reinforce. Refer to the chart on page 5 to locate the desired cards. War! and Concentration use 24 game cards each, while Go Fish! uses 48 cards. Copy, laminate, and cut out the cards, and the game's ready to be played—it's that simple! You can store the game cards for each game in a resealable plastic bag labeled with the name of the game and the featured skills.

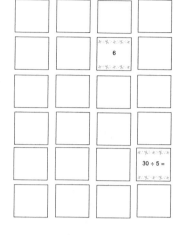

Tic-Tac-Toe

Choose the version of this game that you'd like students to play. Then select the game cards that correspond to the facts you want to feature in the game (refer to the chart on page 5). Copy the Tic-Tac-Toe game board on page 16 and one set of game markers (page 35) on green paper and another set on blue paper. Laminate and cut out all the game pieces. Then store them in a large resealable plastic bag labeled with the name of the game and the targeted skills.

Checkers

To prepare each Checkers game board, you'll need a 12- by 18-inch sheet of construction paper and glue. Copy and cut out the two parts of the game board (either pages 44–45 or 46–47), glue them together where indicated, and glue the entire game board to the construction paper. Then copy one set of game markers (page 35) onto red paper and another set onto yellow paper. Laminate the game board and game markers, and cut out the markers. To store, label a resealable plastic bag with the name of the game. Place the markers in the bag along with a wipe-off marker and paper towels. Then attach the bag to the game board with a paper clip.

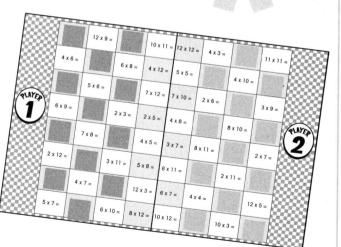

To introduce the different versions of each game, play the game with students or assist them as they play. For games that require turn-taking, help students establish a method for determining the order in which they will take turns, such as by taking turns in the order of their birthdays.

Bingo

2 or more
plus a caller

Choose a Version to Play

x Multiplication practice: To match products, use the targeted multiplication cards on the game boards and the corresponding caller recording charts on pages 36–39 (the caller calls out the products shown in the circles). To match facts, use the targeted product number cards on the game boards and the corresponding caller recording charts on pages 36–39 (the caller calls out the multiplication facts).

÷ Division practice: To match quotients, use the targeted division cards on the game boards and the corresponding caller recording charts on pages 40–43 (the caller calls out the quotients shown in the circles). To match facts, use the quotient number cards on the game boards and the corresponding caller recording charts on pages 40–43 (the caller calls out the division facts).

Materials

- 1 game board per player
- Caller recording charts
- 12 game markers per player (page 35)
- Wipe-off pen
- Paper towels

How to Play

1. Each player selects a game board and takes 12 game markers.

2. The caller calls out an item on a caller recording chart. He or she marks that item with the wipe-off pen. If the caller calls out a product or quotient, he or she should mark that number anytime it appears on any of the charts in use.

3. Players check their game boards to see if any spaces show a match to the called item. If a player finds a match, he or she places a marker on the space. If the player has more than one matching item, he or she places a marker on each matching space.

4. Play continues with the caller calling out one item at a time and players searching their game boards for matches. The first player to cover four spaces in a row—across, down, or diagonally— calls "Bingo!" Then the player and caller compare each answer on the game board to the marked items on the caller recording charts to check for correctness. If all the answers are correct, the player wins the game.

Challenge

Reinforce the inverse property of multiplication and division. Give each player a multiplication game board. To play, the caller names facts from the corresponding division caller recording charts. Players search their game boards and mark each space with a matching multiplication fact. For example, if the caller calls 63 ÷ 9, players cover 9 x 7 or 7 x 9.

OBJECTIVE

To answer multiplication or division facts and be the first player to cover four spaces in a row on his or her game board

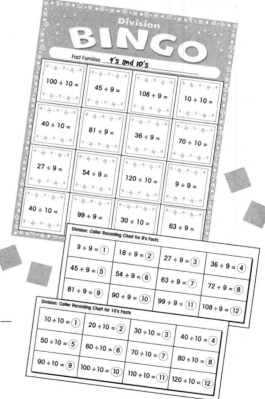

Variation

Instead of four in a row, have players cover all the spaces on their game board to win. Or play speed Bingo by calling out one item after another in quick succession.

War!

Choose a Version to Play

x Multiplication practice with facts: Use 24 multiplication cards for the targeted fact families.

x Multiplication practice with facts and products: Use the 12 multiplication cards for the targeted fact family and the 12 corresponding product number cards.

÷ Division practice with facts: Use 24 division cards for the targeted fact families.

÷ Division practice with facts and quotients: Use the 12 division cards for the targeted fact family and the 12 quotient number cards (page 35).

Materials

• 24 game cards

How to Play

1. One player shuffles the cards and deals them evenly between the players. Each player stacks his or her cards facedown.

2. Each player turns over the top card on his or her stack. Then each player announces the answer to the fact or names the number shown on his or her card. The player with the card that equals the higher value takes both cards and puts them facedown on the bottom of his or her stack.

   ❋ If both cards have the same value, the players call out "War!" Then each player turns over the next card in his or her stack. The player with the war card that has the higher value wins the war. That player collects all the cards in play.

   ❋ If both war cards have the same value, players continue the war by turning over the next card in their stacks. The war ends when one player turns over a card with a higher value than the other player's card.

3. Play continues until one player collects all the cards and ends the game. The player with all the cards wins the game.

Challenge

To emphasize the inverse property of multiplication and division, use a set of related multiplication and division cards (such as the 4's fact family). To play, players compare the products of multiplication facts to the divisors of division facts. If different, the higher number wins the round. If the same, war is declared. If both cards have either multiplication facts or division facts, the card with the higher value wins the round.

OBJECTIVE

To compute and compare answers to multiplication or division facts and be the player to end the game by collecting all the cards

Variation

For 3–4 players, use four sets of game cards featuring the facts of your choice. Deal the 48 game cards evenly among the players. Whenever two or more players turn over cards that have the same value, each of those players participates in the war to break the tie.

Go Fish! •••••••••••••••••••••••••••••••••

Choose a Version to Play

✗ Multiplication practice with facts and products: Use 24 multiplication cards for the targeted fact families and the 24 corresponding product number cards.

÷ Division practice with facts and quotients: Use 24 division cards for the targeted fact families and two sets of the 12 quotient number cards (page 35).

Materials

• 48 game cards

How to Play

1. One player shuffles the cards and deals five cards to each player. He or she stacks the remaining cards facedown on the table.

2. The first player checks his or her cards for any matching cards. A match can be made if a fact card has the same value as a number card (such as 2 x 6 and 12), two fact cards have the same answer (such as 1 x 4 and 2 x 2), or two number cards have the same value (such as 8 and 8). If the player has two or more cards that equal the same value, he or she shows the match to the other players and places it on the table.

3. The first player then calls out a fact or number card in his or her hand. The player names another player and asks him or her for any matching cards.

 ✳ If the named player has one or more matching cards, he or she must give all of those cards to the asking player. That player then lays the new match on the table and takes another turn.

 ✳ If the named player does not have any matching cards, he or she says "Go Fish." Then the asking player takes the top card in the stack, adds it to his or her hand, and the turn ends.

4. Players continue to take turns. The game ends when a player uses all the cards in his or her hand or no more matches can be made. To score, each player counts the sets of matching cards he or she has on the table. The player with the most sets of matches wins.

Challenge

Use 24 multiplication cards and the 24 related division cards. To play, a player calls out a fact and asks another player for a matching inverse fact. For example, a player might call out 6 x 4. If the asked player holds a card with 24 ÷ 6 or 24 ÷ 4 , he or she gives the card to the asking player.

OBJECTIVE

To solve multiplication or division facts and be the player with the most sets of matching cards at the end of the game

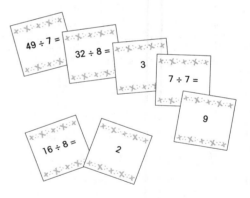

Variation

Make two copies of the same set of fact cards. To play, players request cards by naming the answer to the fact on a card in his or her hand.

Concentration

Choose a Version to Play

x Multiplication practice with facts and products: Use the 12 multiplication cards for the targeted fact family and the 12 corresponding product number cards.

÷ Division practice with facts and quotients: Use the 12 division cards for the targeted fact family and the 12 quotient number cards (page 35).

Materials

• 24 game cards

How to Play

1. Players place the game cards facedown on the table in a four-by-six array.

2. The first player turns over any two cards and checks to see if the cards form a match. A match can be made only when a player turns over a fact card and a number card. If the answer to the fact equals the number on the other card, a match is made. If a player turns over two fact cards or two number cards, the turn ends and the player returns the cards facedown to their positions on the table.

⁕ If the player finds a match, he or she keeps the cards and takes another turn.

⁕ If the player does not find a match, he or she returns the cards facedown to the table and the turn ends.

3. Players continue to take turns until all the matches have been made. At the end of the game, each player counts his or her matches. The player with the most matches wins the game.

Challenge

Play this version of the game to reinforce the inverse property of multiplication and division. Place 12 multiplication fact cards and the 12 related division fact cards facedown on the table. Players turn over two cards at a time. If both cards show either multiplication facts or division facts, the player returns the cards to the table and the turn ends. If one card shows a multiplication fact and the other a division fact, the player decides whether or not the two facts are related (such as 7 x 9 and 63 ÷ 9). If so, the player keeps the cards and takes another turn. If not, the player returns the cards to the table.

OBJECTIVE

To match multiplication or division facts to the correct answers and be the player with the most matches at the end of the game

Variation

To add interest, tell players that matches can also be made if two facts cards have the same answer (such as 1 x 4 and 2 x 2) or two number cards have the same value (such as 8 and 8).

Tic-Tac-Toe

Choose a Version to Play

x Multiplication practice with facts: Use three sets of multiplication cards for the targeted fact family (three copies of the same set of cards or three different sets of cards can be used).

÷ Division practice with facts: Use three sets of division cards for the targeted fact family (three copies of the same set of cards or three different sets of cards can be used).

Materials

- 36 game cards
- Tic-Tac-Toe game board (page 16)
- 5 green game markers (page 35)
- 5 blue game markers (page 35)

How to Play

1. One player shuffles the cards and then places one card facedown on each square on the game board. The player sets the remaining stack of cards aside for later use. Each player selects a set of game markers.

2. The first player turns over a card, reads the fact, and gives the answer. If the player answers correctly, he or she places a marker on that card and the turn ends. If the player's answer is incorrect, the turn ends. The second player may choose to answer that fact or turn over another card. If he or she chooses to turn over another card, the first one is returned facedown to its space.

3. Players continue taking turns until one player places his or her markers on three cards in a row—across, down, or diagonally—or until all the cards have been turned over and the facts answered correctly. If a player marks three cards in a row, he or she wins the round. If neither player marks three cards in a row, the round results in a tie.

4. After completing the round, players collect their markers and remove the cards from the game board. They then use nine more cards from the stack to set up the game board for another round of play. (There are enough cards for players to play four rounds of Tic-Tac-Toe.)

Challenge

Have players answer each fact with a related fact from the inverse operation. For example, if a player turns over a card with 3 x 4, he or she should answer with a related division fact, such as 12 ÷ 3 or 12 ÷ 4.

OBJECTIVE

To correctly answer multiplication or division facts and be the first player to cover three squares in a row on the Tic-Tac-Toe game board

Variation

Have players answer each fact with an equivalent fact of the same operation. For example, the player might answer 3 x 3 with 1 x 9.

Checkers

Choose a Version to Play

x Players find the answers to multiplication facts: Use the multiplication Checkers game board (pages 44–45).

÷ Players find the answers to division facts: Use the division Checkers game board (pages 46–47).

Materials

- Checkers game board
- 12 red game markers (page 35)
- 12 yellow game markers (page 35)
- Wipe-off pen
- Paper towels

> ### OBJECTIVE
>
> To answer multiplication or division facts and be the first player to either capture all the opponent's markers or prevent him or her from making any more moves

How to Play

1. Each player selects one side of the game board and a set of markers. The player places a marker on each shaded space on the first three rows of his or her side of the game board.

2. The first player moves one of his or her markers forward diagonally to a shaded space without a marker. The player reads and answers the fact on that space. If correct, the player leaves the marker on the space and the turn ends. If incorrect, the player returns the marker to its original space and the turn ends.

3. Players take turns moving their markers. When a player moves to a space that touches the corner of a space holding the opponent's marker, the player may try to capture that marker—but only if the space on the opposite corner does not hold a marker. To do this, the player jumps his or her marker over the opponent's marker to the space without a marker. Then the player answers the fact on that space and all the facts on the surrounding white spaces.

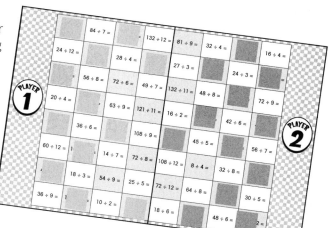

　*　If the player answers all the facts correctly, he or she captures the opponent's marker by removing it from the board. Then the turn ends.

　*　If the player does not answer all the facts correctly, the capture does not take place. The player moves his or her marker back to its original space, and the turn ends.

4. When a player moves one of his or her markers to the last row on the opposite side of the game board, and then correctly answers the fact on that space and any surrounding white spaces, the marker may be crowned a king. To do this, the player writes a *K* on the marker. Players may move their kings forward or backward. To capture an opponent's marker with a king, players must follow the capture rule in Step 3.

5. Play continues until one player wins by either capturing all of his or her opponent's markers or preventing the opponent from making any more moves. When finished, players clean their game markers with a paper towel for use again in future games.

Multiplication BINGO

Fact Families _____

Math Games to Master Basic Skills: Multiplication & Division Scholastic Teaching Resources

Division Bingo Game Board

Division

BINGO

Fact Families _____

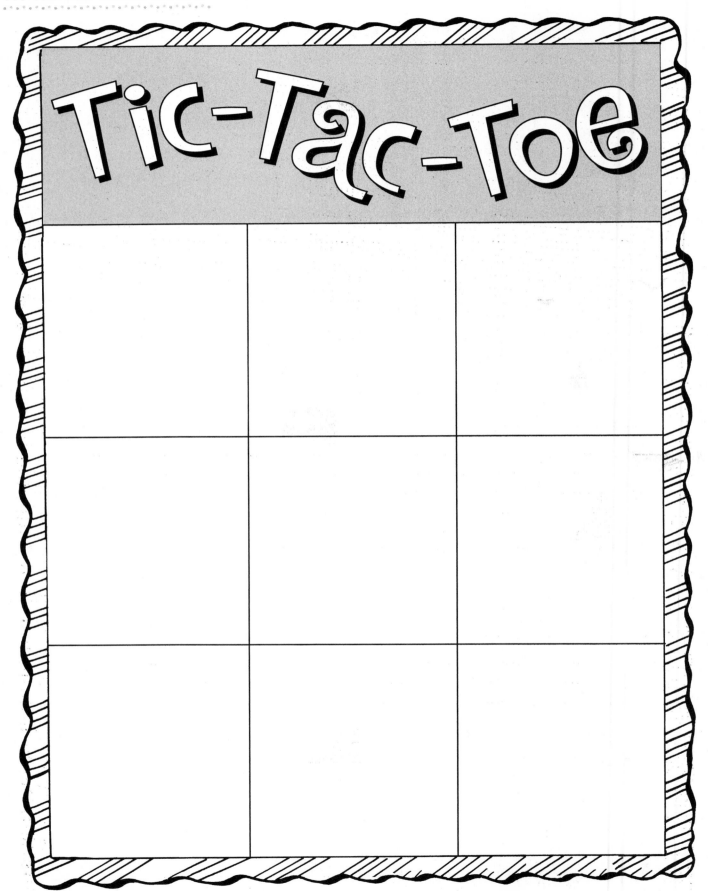

Math Games to Master Basic Skills: Multiplication & Division Scholastic Teaching Resources

Multiplication Game Cards: 1's Facts

1 x 1 =	1 x 2 =	1 x 3 =	1 x 4 =
1 x 5 =	1 x 6 =	1 x 7 =	1 x 8 =
1 x 9 =	1 x 10 =	1 x 11 =	1 x 12 =

Multiplication Game Cards: 2's Facts

2 x 1 =	2 x 2 =	2 x 3 =	2 x 4 =
2 x 5 =	2 x 6 =	2 x 7 =	2 x 8 =
2 x 9 =	2 x 10 =	2 x 11 =	2 x 12 =

Multiplication Game Cards: 3's Facts

3 x 1 =	3 x 2 =	3 x 3 =	3 x 4 =
3 x 5 =	3 x 6 =	3 x 7 =	3 x 8 =
3 x 9 =	3 x 10 =	3 x 11 =	3 x 12 =

Multiplication Game Cards: 4's Facts

4 x 1 =	4 x 2 =	4 x 3 =	4 x 4 =
4 x 5 =	4 x 6 =	4 x 7 =	4 x 8 =
4 x 9 =	4 x 10 =	4 x 11 =	4 x 12 =

Math Games to Master Basic Skills: Multiplication & Division   Scholastic Teaching Resources

Multiplication Game Cards: 5's Facts

5 x 1 =	5 x 2 =	5 x 3 =	5 x 4 =
5 x 5 =	5 x 6 =	5 x 7 =	5 x 8 =
5 x 9 =	5 x 10 =	5 x 11 =	5 x 12 =

Multiplication Game Cards: 6's Facts

6 x 1 =	6 x 2 =	6 x 3 =	6 x 4 =
6 x 5 =	6 x 6 =	6 x 7 =	6 x 8 =
6 x 9 =	6 x 10 =	6 x 11 =	6 x 12 =

Multiplication Game Cards: 7's Facts

7 x 1 =	7 x 2 =	7 x 3 =	7 x 4 =
7 x 5 =	7 x 6 =	7 x 7 =	7 x 8 =
7 x 9 =	7 x 10 =	7 x 11 =	7 x 12 =

Multiplication Game Cards: 8's Facts

8 x 1 =	8 x 2 =	8 x 3 =	8 x 4 =
8 x 5 =	8 x 6 =	8 x 7 =	8 x 8 =
8 x 9 =	8 x 10 =	8 x 11 =	8 x 12 =

Math Games to Master Basic Skills: Multiplication & Division Scholastic Teaching Resources

Multiplication Game Cards: 9's Facts

9 x 1 =	9 x 2 =	9 x 3 =	9 x 4 =
9 x 5 =	9 x 6 =	9 x 7 =	9 x 8 =
9 x 9 =	9 x 10 =	9 x 11 =	9 x 12 =

Multiplication Game Cards: 10's Facts

10 x 1 =	10 x 2 =	10 x 3 =	10 x 4 =
10 x 5 =	10 x 6 =	10 x 7 =	10 x 8 =
10 x 9 =	10 x 10 =	10 x 11 =	10 x 12 =

Multiplication Game Cards: 11's Facts

11 x 1 =	11 x 2 =	11 x 3 =	11 x 4 =
11 x 5 =	11 x 6 =	11 x 7 =	11 x 8 =
11 x 9 =	11 x 10 =	11 x 11 =	11 x 12 =

Multiplication Game Cards: 12's Facts

12 x 1 =	12 x 2 =	12 x 3 =	12 x 4 =
12 x 5 =	12 x 6 =	12 x 7 =	12 x 8 =
12 x 9 =	12 x 10 =	12 x 11 =	12 x 12 =

Math Games to Master Basic Skills: Multiplication & Division Scholastic Teaching Resources

Multiplication Game Cards: Products for 1's Facts

1	2	3	4
5	6	7	8
9	10	11	12

Multiplication Game Cards: Products for 2's Facts

2	4	6	8
10	12	14	16
18	20	22	24

Multiplication Game Cards: Products for 3's Facts

3	6	9	12
15	18	21	24
27	30	33	36

Multiplication Game Cards: Products for 4's Facts

4	8	12	16
20	24	28	32
36	40	44	48

Math Games to Master Basic Skills: Multiplication & Division Scholastic Teaching Resources

Multiplication Game Cards: Products for 5's Facts

5	10	15	20
25	30	35	40
45	50	55	60

Multiplication Game Cards: Products for 6's Facts

6	12	18	24
30	36	42	48
54	60	66	72

Multiplication Game Cards: Products for 7's Facts

7	14	21	28
35	42	49	56
63	70	77	84

Multiplication Game Cards: Products for 8's Facts

8	16	24	32
40	48	56	64
72	80	88	96

26

Math Games to Master Basic Skills: Multiplication & Division   Scholastic Teaching Resources

Multiplication Game Cards: Products for 9's Facts

9	18	27	36
45	54	63	72
81	90	99	108

Multiplication Game Cards: Products for 10's Facts

10	20	30	40
50	60	70	80
90	100	110	120

Multiplication Game Cards: Products for 11's Facts

11	22	33	44
55	66	77	88
99	110	121	132

Multiplication Game Cards: Products for 12's Facts

12	24	36	48
60	72	84	96
108	120	132	144

Math Games to Master Basic Skills: Multiplication & Division   Scholastic Teaching Resources

Division Game Cards: 1's Facts

$1 \div 1 =$	$2 \div 1 =$	$3 \div 1 =$	$4 \div 1 =$
$5 \div 1 =$	$6 \div 1 =$	$7 \div 1 =$	$8 \div 1 =$
$9 \div 1 =$	$10 \div 1 =$	$11 \div 1 =$	$12 \div 1 =$

Division Game Cards: 2's Facts

$2 \div 2 =$	$4 \div 2 =$	$6 \div 2 =$	$8 \div 2 =$
$10 \div 2 =$	$12 \div 2 =$	$14 \div 2 =$	$16 \div 2 =$
$18 \div 2 =$	$20 \div 2 =$	$22 \div 2 =$	$24 \div 2 =$

Division Game Cards: 3's Facts

3 ÷ 3 =	6 ÷ 3 =	9 ÷ 3 =	12 ÷ 3 =
15 ÷ 3 =	18 ÷ 3 =	21 ÷ 3 =	24 ÷ 3 =
27 ÷ 3 =	30 ÷ 3 =	33 ÷ 3 =	36 ÷ 3 =

Division Game Cards: 4's Facts

4 ÷ 4 =	8 ÷ 4 =	12 ÷ 4 =	16 ÷ 4 =
20 ÷ 4 =	24 ÷ 4 =	28 ÷ 4 =	32 ÷ 4 =
36 ÷ 4 =	40 ÷ 4 =	44 ÷ 4 =	48 ÷ 4 =

Math Games to Master Basic Skills: Multiplication & Division Scholastic Teaching Resources

Division Game Cards: 5's Facts

5 ÷ 5 =	10 ÷ 5 =	15 ÷ 5 =	20 ÷ 5 =
25 ÷ 5 =	30 ÷ 5 =	35 ÷ 5 =	40 ÷ 5 =
45 ÷ 5 =	50 ÷ 5 =	55 ÷ 5 =	60 ÷ 5 =

Division Game Cards: 6's Facts

6 ÷ 6 =	12 ÷ 6 =	18 ÷ 6 =	24 ÷ 6 =
30 ÷ 6 =	36 ÷ 6 =	42 ÷ 6 =	48 ÷ 6 =
54 ÷ 6 =	60 ÷ 6 =	66 ÷ 6 =	72 ÷ 6 =

Division Game Cards: 7's Facts

$7 \div 7 =$	$14 \div 7 =$	$21 \div 7 =$	$28 \div 7 =$
$35 \div 7 =$	$42 \div 7 =$	$49 \div 7 =$	$56 \div 7 =$
$63 \div 7 =$	$70 \div 7 =$	$77 \div 7 =$	$84 \div 7 =$

Division Game Cards: 8's Facts

$8 \div 8 =$	$16 \div 8 =$	$24 \div 8 =$	$32 \div 8 =$
$40 \div 8 =$	$48 \div 8 =$	$56 \div 8 =$	$64 \div 8 =$
$72 \div 8 =$	$80 \div 8 =$	$88 \div 8 =$	$96 \div 8 =$

Math Games to Master Basic Skills: Multiplication & Division Scholastic Teaching Resources

Division Game Cards: 9's Facts

$9 \div 9 =$	$18 \div 9 =$	$27 \div 9 =$	$36 \div 9 =$
$45 \div 9 =$	$54 \div 9 =$	$63 \div 9 =$	$72 \div 9 =$
$81 \div 9 =$	$90 \div 9 =$	$99 \div 9 =$	$108 \div 9 =$

Division Game Cards: 10's Facts

$10 \div 10 =$	$20 \div 10 =$	$30 \div 10 =$	$40 \div 10 =$
$50 \div 10 =$	$60 \div 10 =$	$70 \div 10 =$	$80 \div 10 =$
$90 \div 10 =$	$100 \div 10 =$	$110 \div 10 =$	$120 \div 10 =$

Division Game Cards: 11's Facts

11 ÷ 11 =	22 ÷ 11 =	33 ÷ 11 =	44 ÷ 11 =
55 ÷ 11 =	66 ÷ 11 =	77 ÷ 11 =	88 ÷ 11 =
99 ÷ 11 =	110 ÷ 11 =	121 ÷ 11 =	132 ÷ 11 =

Division Game Cards: 12's Facts

12 ÷ 12 =	24 ÷ 12 =	36 ÷ 12 =	48 ÷ 12 =
60 ÷ 12 =	72 ÷ 12 =	84 ÷ 12 =	96 ÷ 12 =
108 ÷ 12 =	120 ÷ 12 =	132 ÷ 12 =	144 ÷ 12 =

Math Games to Master Basic Skills: Multiplication & Division Scholastic Teaching Resources

Division Game Cards: Quotients

1	2	3	4
5	6	7	8
9	10	11	12

Game Markers

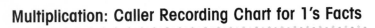

Multiplication: Caller Recording Chart for 1's Facts

1 x 1 = ①	1 x 2 = ②	1 x 3 = ③	1 x 4 = ④
1 x 5 = ⑤	1 x 6 = ⑥	1 x 7 = ⑦	1 x 8 = ⑧
1 x 9 = ⑨	1 x 10 = ⑩	1 x 11 = ⑪	1 x 12 = ⑫

Multiplication: Caller Recording Chart for 2's Facts

2 x 1 = ②	2 x 2 = ④	2 x 3 = ⑥	2 x 4 = ⑧
2 x 5 = ⑩	2 x 6 = ⑫	2 x 7 = ⑭	2 x 8 = ⑯
2 x 9 = ⑱	2 x 10 = ⑳	2 x 11 = ㉒	2 x 12 = ㉔

Multiplication: Caller Recording Chart for 3's Facts

3 x 1 = ③	3 x 2 = ⑥	3 x 3 = ⑨	3 x 4 = ⑫
3 x 5 = ⑮	3 x 6 = ⑱	3 x 7 = ㉑	3 x 8 = ㉔
3 x 9 = ㉗	3 x 10 = ㉚	3 x 11 = ㉝	3 x 12 = ㊱

Math Games to Master Basic Skills: Multiplication & Division Scholastic Teaching Resources

Multiplication: Caller Recording Chart for 4's Facts

4 x 1 = (4)	4 x 2 = (8)	4 x 3 = (12)	4 x 4 = (16)
4 x 5 = (20)	4 x 6 = (24)	4 x 7 = (28)	4 x 8 = (32)
4 x 9 = (36)	4 x 10 = (40)	4 x 11 = (44)	4 x 12 = (48)

Multiplication: Caller Recording Chart for 5's Facts

5 x 1 = (5)	5 x 2 = (10)	5 x 3 = (15)	5 x 4 = (20)
5 x 5 = (25)	5 x 6 = (30)	5 x 7 = (35)	5 x 8 = (40)
5 x 9 = (45)	5 x 10 = (50)	5 x 11 = (55)	5 x 12 = (60)

Multiplication: Caller Recording Chart for 6's Facts

6 x 1 = (6)	6 x 2 = (12)	6 x 3 = (18)	6 x 4 = (24)
6 x 5 = (30)	6 x 6 = (36)	6 x 7 = (42)	6 x 8 = (48)
6 x 9 = (54)	6 x 10 = (60)	6 x 11 = (66)	6 x 12 = (72)

Multiplication: Caller Recording Chart for 7's Facts

7 x 1 = 7	7 x 2 = 14	7 x 3 = 21	7 x 4 = 28
7 x 5 = 35	7 x 6 = 42	7 x 7 = 49	7 x 8 = 56
7 x 9 = 63	7 x 10 = 70	7 x 11 = 77	7 x 12 = 84

Multiplication: Caller Recording Chart for 8's Facts

8 x 1 = 8	8 x 2 = 16	8 x 3 = 24	8 x 4 = 32
8 x 5 = 40	8 x 6 = 48	8 x 7 = 56	8 x 8 = 64
8 x 9 = 72	8 x 10 = 80	8 x 11 = 88	8 x 12 = 96

Multiplication: Caller Recording Chart for 9's Facts

9 x 1 = 9	9 x 2 = 18	9 x 3 = 27	9 x 4 = 36
9 x 5 = 45	9 x 6 = 54	9 x 7 = 63	9 x 8 = 72
9 x 9 = 81	9 x 10 = 90	9 x 11 = 99	9 x 12 = 108

Multiplication: Caller Recording Chart for 10's Facts

10 x 1 = (10)	10 x 2 = (20)	10 x 3 = (30)	10 x 4 = (40)
10 x 5 = (50)	10 x 6 = (60)	10 x 7 = (70)	10 x 8 = (80)
10 x 9 = (90)	10 x 10 = (100)	10 x 11 = (110)	10 x 12 = (120)

Multiplication: Caller Recording Chart for 11's Facts

11 x 1 = (11)	11 x 2 = (22)	11 x 3 = (33)	11 x 4 = (44)
11 x 5 = (55)	11 x 6 = (66)	11 x 7 = (77)	11 x 8 = (88)
11 x 9 = (99)	11 x 10 = (110)	11 x 11 = (121)	11 x 12 = (132)

Multiplication: Caller Recording Chart for 12's Facts

12 x 1 = (12)	12 x 2 = (24)	12 x 3 = (36)	12 x 4 = (48)
12 x 5 = (60)	12 x 6 = (72)	12 x 7 = (84)	12 x 8 = (96)
12 x 9 = (108)	12 x 10 = (120)	12 x 11 = (132)	12 x 12 = (144)

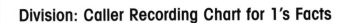

Division: Caller Recording Chart for 1's Facts

$1 \div 1 =$ ①	$2 \div 1 =$ ②	$3 \div 1 =$ ③	$4 \div 1 =$ ④
$5 \div 1 =$ ⑤	$6 \div 1 =$ ⑥	$7 \div 1 =$ ⑦	$8 \div 1 =$ ⑧
$9 \div 1 =$ ⑨	$10 \div 1 =$ ⑩	$11 \div 1 =$ ⑪	$12 \div 1 =$ ⑫

Division: Caller Recording Chart for 2's Facts

$2 \div 2 =$ ①	$4 \div 2 =$ ②	$6 \div 2 =$ ③	$8 \div 2 =$ ④
$10 \div 2 =$ ⑤	$12 \div 2 =$ ⑥	$14 \div 2 =$ ⑦	$16 \div 2 =$ ⑧
$18 \div 2 =$ ⑨	$20 \div 2 =$ ⑩	$22 \div 2 =$ ⑪	$24 \div 2 =$ ⑫

Division: Caller Recording Chart for 3's Facts

$3 \div 3 =$ ①	$6 \div 3 =$ ②	$9 \div 3 =$ ③	$12 \div 3 =$ ④
$15 \div 3 =$ ⑤	$18 \div 3 =$ ⑥	$21 \div 3 =$ ⑦	$24 \div 3 =$ ⑧
$27 \div 3 =$ ⑨	$30 \div 3 =$ ⑩	$33 \div 3 =$ ⑪	$36 \div 3 =$ ⑫

 Math Games to Master Basic Skills: Multiplication & Division Scholastic Teaching Resources

Division: Caller Recording Chart for 4's Facts

4 ÷ 4 = ①	8 ÷ 4 = ②	12 ÷ 4 = ③	16 ÷ 4 = ④
20 ÷ 4 = ⑤	24 ÷ 4 = ⑥	28 ÷ 4 = ⑦	32 ÷ 4 = ⑧
36 ÷ 4 = ⑨	40 ÷ 4 = ⑩	44 ÷ 4 = ⑪	48 ÷ 4 = ⑫

Division: Caller Recording Chart for 5's Facts

5 ÷ 5 = ①	10 ÷ 5 = ②	15 ÷ 5 = ③	20 ÷ 5 = ④
25 ÷ 5 = ⑤	30 ÷ 5 = ⑥	35 ÷ 5 = ⑦	40 ÷ 5 = ⑧
45 ÷ 5 = ⑨	50 ÷ 5 = ⑩	55 ÷ 5 = ⑪	60 ÷ 5 = ⑫

Division: Caller Recording Chart for 6's Facts

6 ÷ 6 = ①	12 ÷ 6 = ②	18 ÷ 6 = ③	24 ÷ 6 = ④
30 ÷ 6 = ⑤	36 ÷ 6 = ⑥	42 ÷ 6 = ⑦	48 ÷ 6 = ⑧
54 ÷ 6 = ⑨	60 ÷ 6 = ⑩	66 ÷ 6 = ⑪	72 ÷ 6 = ⑫

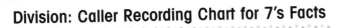

Division: Caller Recording Chart for 7's Facts

$7 \div 7 =$ ⓵	$14 \div 7 =$ ②	$21 \div 7 =$ ③	$28 \div 7 =$ ④
$35 \div 7 =$ ⑤	$42 \div 7 =$ ⑥	$49 \div 7 =$ ⑦	$56 \div 7 =$ ⑧
$63 \div 7 =$ ⑨	$70 \div 7 =$ ⑩	$77 \div 7 =$ ⑪	$84 \div 7 =$ ⑫

Division: Caller Recording Chart for 8's Facts

$8 \div 8 =$ ⓵	$16 \div 8 =$ ②	$24 \div 8 =$ ③	$32 \div 8 =$ ④
$40 \div 8 =$ ⑤	$48 \div 8 =$ ⑥	$56 \div 8 =$ ⑦	$64 \div 8 =$ ⑧
$72 \div 8 =$ ⑨	$80 \div 8 =$ ⑩	$88 \div 8 =$ ⑪	$96 \div 8 =$ ⑫

Division: Caller Recording Chart for 9's Facts

$9 \div 9 =$ ⓵	$18 \div 9 =$ ②	$27 \div 9 =$ ③	$36 \div 9 =$ ④
$45 \div 9 =$ ⑤	$54 \div 9 =$ ⑥	$63 \div 9 =$ ⑦	$72 \div 9 =$ ⑧
$81 \div 9 =$ ⑨	$90 \div 9 =$ ⑩	$99 \div 9 =$ ⑪	$108 \div 9 =$ ⑫

Math Games to Master Basic Skills: Multiplication & Division Scholastic Teaching Resources

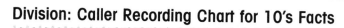

Division: Caller Recording Chart for 10's Facts

10 ÷ 10 = ①	20 ÷ 10 = ②	30 ÷ 10 = ③	40 ÷ 10 = ④
50 ÷ 10 = ⑤	60 ÷ 10 = ⑥	70 ÷ 10 = ⑦	80 ÷ 10 = ⑧
90 ÷ 10 = ⑨	100 ÷ 10 = ⑩	110 ÷ 10 = ⑪	120 ÷ 10 = ⑫

Division: Caller Recording Chart for 11's Facts

11 ÷ 11 = ①	22 ÷ 11 = ②	33 ÷ 11 = ③	44 ÷ 11 = ④
55 ÷ 11 = ⑤	66 ÷ 11 = ⑥	77 ÷ 11 = ⑦	88 ÷ 11 = ⑧
99 ÷ 11 = ⑨	110 ÷ 11 = ⑩	121 ÷ 11 = ⑪	132 ÷ 11 = ⑫

Division: Caller Recording Chart for 12's Facts

12 ÷ 12 = ①	24 ÷ 12 = ②	36 ÷ 12 = ③	48 ÷ 12 = ④
60 ÷ 12 = ⑤	72 ÷ 12 = ⑥	84 ÷ 12 = ⑦	96 ÷ 12 = ⑧
108 ÷ 12 = ⑨	120 ÷ 12 = ⑩	132 ÷ 12 = ⑪	144 ÷ 12 = ⑫

Checkers Game Board: Multiplication

8 x 3 =	12 x 9 =	5 x 10 =	10 x 11 =
4 x 6 =	7 x 9 =	6 x 8 =	4 x 12 =
4 x 9 =	5 x 6 =	3 x 3 =	7 x 12 =
6 x 9 =	7 x 7 =	2 x 3 =	2 x 5 =
2 x 2 =	7 x 8 =	6 x 12 =	4 x 5 =
2 x 12 =	8 x 9 =	3 x 11 =	5 x 8 =
3 x 5 =	4 x 7 =	2 x 9 =	12 x 3 =
5 x 7 =	7 x 11 =	6 x 10 =	8 x 12 =

PLAYER 1

Math Games to Master Basic Skills: Multiplication & Division Scholastic Teaching Resources

Checkers Game Board: Multiplication

12 x 12 =	4 x 3 =	8 x 8 =	11 x 11 =
5 x 5 =	7 x 3 =	4 x 10 =	11 x 12 =
7 x 10 =	2 x 6 =	6 x 6 =	3 x 9 =
4 x 8 =	5 x 11 =	8 x 10 =	2 x 9 =
3 x 7 =	8 x 11 =	5 x 9 =	2 x 7 =
6 x 11 =	3 x 6 =	2 x 11 =	4 x 11 =
6 x 7 =	4 x 4 =	2 x 8 =	12 x 5 =
10 x 12 =	2 x 4 =	10 x 3 =	9 x 9 =

PLAYER 2

Glue here.

Checkers Game Board: Division

<table>
<tr><td>$24 \div 6 =$</td><td>$84 \div 7 =$</td><td>$88 \div 11 =$</td><td>$132 \div 12 =$</td></tr>
<tr><td>$24 \div 12 =$</td><td>$9 \div 3 =$</td><td>$28 \div 4 =$</td><td>$21 \div 3 =$</td></tr>
<tr><td>$35 \div 7 =$</td><td>$56 \div 8 =$</td><td>$72 \div 6 =$</td><td>$49 \div 7 =$</td></tr>
<tr><td>$20 \div 4 =$</td><td>$54 \div 6 =$</td><td>$63 \div 9 =$</td><td>$121 \div 11 =$</td></tr>
<tr><td>$15 \div 5 =$</td><td>$36 \div 6 =$</td><td>$18 \div 9 =$</td><td>$108 \div 9 =$</td></tr>
<tr><td>$60 \div 12 =$</td><td>$100 \div 10 =$</td><td>$14 \div 7 =$</td><td>$72 \div 8 =$</td></tr>
<tr><td>$48 \div 4 =$</td><td>$18 \div 3 =$</td><td>$54 \div 9 =$</td><td>$25 \div 5 =$</td></tr>
<tr><td>$36 \div 9 =$</td><td>$110 \div 11 =$</td><td>$10 \div 2 =$</td><td>$6 \div 3 =$</td></tr>
</table>

PLAYER 1

Math Games to Master Basic Skills: Multiplication & Division   Scholastic Teaching Resources

Glue here.

81 ÷ 9 =	32 ÷ 4 =	12 ÷ 6 =	16 ÷ 4 =
27 ÷ 3 =	20 ÷ 5 =	24 ÷ 3 =	144 ÷ 12 =
132 ÷ 11 =	48 ÷ 8 =	36 ÷ 3 =	72 ÷ 9 =
16 ÷ 2 =	28 ÷ 7 =	42 ÷ 6 =	40 ÷ 5 =
63 ÷ 7 =	45 ÷ 5 =	70 ÷ 10 =	56 ÷ 7 =
108 ÷ 12 =	8 ÷ 4 =	32 ÷ 8 =	77 ÷ 7 =
72 ÷ 12 =	64 ÷ 8 =	12 ÷ 4 =	30 ÷ 5 =
18 ÷ 6 =	96 ÷ 8 =	48 ÷ 6 =	120 ÷ 12 =

PLAYER 2

Multiplication Checkers Answer Key

PLAYER 1 ... **PLAYER 2**

24	108	50	110	144	12	64	121
24	63	48	48	25	21	40	132
36	30	9	84	70	12	36	27
54	49	6	10	32	55	80	18
4	56	72	20	21	88	45	14
24	72	33	40	66	18	22	44
15	28	18	36	42	16	16	60
35	77	60	96	120	8	30	81

Division Checkers Answer Key

PLAYER 1 ... **PLAYER 2**

4	12	8	11	9	8	2	4
2	3	7	7	9	4	8	12
5	7	12	7	12	6	12	8
5	9	7	11	8	4	7	8
3	6	2	12	9	9	7	8
5	10	2	9	9	2	4	11
12	6	6	5	6	8	3	6
4	10	5	2	3	12	8	10

Math Games to Master Basic Skills: Multiplication & Division   Scholastic Teaching Resources